FOR THE
TOUGH TIMES

Reaching Toward Heaven for Hope

MAX LUCADO

THOMAS NELSON
Since 1798

NASHVILLE   DALLAS   MEXICO CITY   RIO DE JANEIRO   BEIJING

FOR THE TOUGH TIMES

Previously published as *For These Tough Times*

© 2006 by Max Lucado

Published in Nashville, Tennessee, by Thomas Nelson. Thomas Nelson is a registered trademark of Thomas Nelson, Inc.

Thomas Nelson, Inc., titles may be purchased in bulk for educational, business, fund-raising, or sales promotional use. For information, please e-mail SpecialMarkets@ThomasNelson.com.

Unless otherwise noted, all Scripture quotations are from The Holy Bible, New Century Version (NCV), © 1987, 1988, 1991 by Word Publishing, Nashville, TN 37214. All rights reserved. Scripture quotations marked (NIV) are taken from the Holy Bible, New International Version® © 1973, 1978, 1984 by International Bible Society. Used by permission of Zondervan Publishing House. All rights reserved. Scripture quotations marked (MSG) are from *The Message.* © by Eugene H. Peterson 1993, 1994, 1995, 1996, 2000, 2001, 2002. Used by permission of NavPress Publishing Group. Scripture quotations marked (NASB) are from the New American Standard Bible® © 1960, 1962, 1963, 1971, 1972, 1973, 1975, 1977, 1995 by The Lockman Foundation. Used by permission. Scripture quotations marked (TLB) are taken from *The Living Bible,* © 1971 by Tyndale House Publishers, Inc., Wheaton, Illinois 60189. All rights reserved. Scripture quotations marked (JB) are from The Jerusalem Bible. © 1966, 1967, 1968 by Darton, Longman & Todd, Ltd. and Doubleday. Scripture quotations marked (KJV) are from the King James Version of the Bible.

Most of the material for this book has been adapted from *America Looks Up, The Great House of God, In the Grip of Grace,* and *When Christ Comes.*

ISBN 978-0-8499-2144-5 (repackage)

The Library of Congress has cataloged the earlier edition as follows:

Lucado, Max.
    For these tough times : reaching toward heaven for hope and healing / Max Lucado.
        p. cm.
Includes bibliographical references.
    ISBN 0-8499-0170-7
    1. Consolation. 2. Spiritual life—Christianity. 3. Prayer—Christianity. I. Title.
    BV4905.3.L84 2006
    248.8'6—dc22

006020559

Printed in the United States of America

08 09 10 11 12 WOR 5 4 3 2 1

For Doug Kostowski,
who cares

CONTENTS

THE BITTER TASTE OF REVENGE

47

IN THE SILENCE, GOD SPEAKS

55

IN THE STORM, WE PRAY

65

FROM GOD'S PERSPECTIVE

71

DO IT AGAIN, LORD

I INTRODUCTION

WHEN ALL THAT IS GOOD FALLS APART

> *"When all that is good falls apart,*
> *what can good people do?"*
> *The LORD is in his holy temple;*
> *the LORD sits on his throne in heaven.*
> —Psalm 11:3–4

Isn't David's question ours? When all that is good falls apart, what can good people do? When illness invades, marriages fail, children suffer, and death strikes, what are we to do?

Curiously, David doesn't answer his question with an answer. He answers it with a declaration: "The LORD is in his holy temple; the LORD sits on his throne in heaven."

His point is unmistakable: God is unaltered by our storms. He is undeterred by our problems. He is unfrightened by these problems. He is in his holy temple. He is on his throne in heaven.

Buildings may fall, careers may crumble, but God does not. Wreckage and rubble have never discouraged him. God has always turned tragedy into triumph.

Did he not do so with Joseph? Look at Joseph in the Egyptian prison. His brothers have sold him out; Potiphar's wife has turned him in. If ever a world has caved in, Joseph's has.

Or consider Moses, watching flocks in the wilderness. Is this what he intended to do with his life? Hardly. His heart beats with Jewish blood.

His passion is to lead the slaves, so why does God have him leading sheep?

And Daniel. What about Daniel? He was among the brightest and best young men of Israel, the equivalent of a West Point cadet or an Ivy Leaguer. But he and his entire generation are being marched out of Jerusalem. The city is destroyed. The Temple is in ruins.

Joseph in prison. Moses in the desert. Daniel in chains. These were dark moments. Who could have seen any good in them? Who could have known that Joseph the prisoner was just one promotion from becoming Joseph the prime minister? Who would have thought that God was giving Moses forty years of wilderness training in the very desert through which he would lead the people? And who could have imagined that Daniel the captive would soon be Daniel the king's counselor?

God does things like that. He did with Joseph,

with Moses, with Daniel, and, most of all, he did with Jesus.

In our toughest times we may see what the followers of Christ saw on the cross. Innocence slaughtered. Goodness murdered. Heaven's tower of strength pierced. Mothers wept, evil danced, and the apostles had to wonder, *When all that is good falls apart, what can good people do?*

God answered their question with a declaration. With the rumble of the earth and the rolling of the rock, he reminded them, "The LORD is in his holy temple; the LORD sits on his throne in heaven."

And, today, we must remember: He still is. He is still in his temple, still on his throne, still in control. And he still makes princes out of prisoners, counselors out of captives, and Sundays out of Fridays. What he did then, he will do still.

It falls to us to ask him to do so.

In these pages we'll ask the questions that trouble

us all during difficult times: Who is our God? Where is God in all of this? Can good come from evil? And prayer—is God really listening? As we ponder these questions together, I pray that God's peace and understanding will touch your heart and bring healing to your spirit.

—MAX LUCADO

WHERE IS GOD?

When tragedy strikes, whether personal, national, or global, people wonder how God could allow such things to happen. What can he be thinking? Is God really in control? Can we trust him to run the universe if he would allow *this*?

It is important to recognize that God dwells in a different realm. He occupies another dimension. "My thoughts are not like your thoughts. Your ways are not like my ways. Just as the heavens are higher than the earth, so are my ways higher than your ways and my thoughts higher than your thoughts" (Isa. 55:8–9).

Make special note of the word *like*. God's thoughts are not our thoughts, nor are they even *like* ours. We aren't even in the same neighborhood. We're thinking, *Preserve the body;* he's thinking, *Save the soul.* We dream of a pay raise. He dreams of raising the dead. We avoid pain and seek peace. God uses pain to bring peace. "I'm going to live before I die," we resolve. "Die so you can live," he instructs. We love what rusts. He loves what endures. We rejoice at our successes. He rejoices at our confessions. We show our children the Nike star with the million-dollar smile and say, "Be like Mike." God points to the crucified carpenter with bloody lips and a torn side and says, "Be like Christ."

Our thoughts are not like God's thoughts. Our ways are not like his ways. He has a different agenda. He dwells in a different dimension. He lives on another plane.

The heavens tell the glory of God,

    and the skies announce what his hands have made.

Day after day they tell the story;

    night after night they tell it again.

They have no speech or words;

    they have no voice to be heard.

But their message goes out through all the world;

    their words go everywhere on earth. (Ps. 19:1–4)

Nature is God's workshop. The sky is his résumé. The universe is his calling card. You want to know who God is? See what he has done. You want to know his power? Take a look at his creation. Curious about his strength? Pay a visit to his home address: 1 Billion Starry Sky Avenue. Want to know his size? Step out into the night and stare at starlight emitted one million years ago, and then read 2 Chronicles 2:6: "No one can really build a house for our God. Not even the highest of heavens can hold him."

> He is untainted by the atmosphere of sin,
>   unbridled by the time line of history,
>   unhindered by the weariness of the body.

What controls you doesn't control him. What troubles you doesn't trouble him. What fatigues you doesn't fatigue him. Is an eagle disturbed by traffic? No, he rises above it. Is the whale perturbed by a hurricane? Of course not; he plunges beneath it. Is the lion flustered by the mouse standing directly in his way? No, he steps over it.

How much more is God able to soar above, plunge beneath, and step over the troubles of the earth! "What is impossible with man is possible with God" (see Matt. 19:26). Our questions betray our lack of understanding:

How can God be everywhere at one time? (Who says God is bound by a body?)

How can God hear all the prayers that come to him? (Perhaps his ears are different from yours.)

How can God be the Father, the Son, and the Holy Spirit? (Could it be that heaven has a different set of physics than earth?)

If people down here won't forgive me, how much more am I guilty before a holy God? (Oh, just the opposite. God is always able to give grace when we humans can't—he invented it.)

How vital that we pray, armed with the knowledge that God is in heaven. Pray with any lesser conviction, and our prayers are timid, shallow, and hollow. Look up and see what God has done, and watch how your prayers are energized.

This knowledge gives us confidence as we face the uncertain future. We know that he is in control of the universe, and so we can rest secure. But also important is the knowledge that this God in heaven has chosen to bend near toward earth to see our sorrow and hear our prayers. He is not so far above us that he is not touched by our tears.

Though we may not be able to see his purpose or his plan, the Lord of heaven is on his throne and in firm control of the universe and our lives. So we entrust him with our future. We entrust him with our very lives.

2 GOD'S GREAT LOVE

It was her singing that did it. At first I didn't notice. Had no reason to. The circumstances were commonplace. A daddy picking up his six-year-old from a Brownie troop meeting. Sara loves Brownies; she loves the awards she earns and the uniform she wears. She'd climbed into the car and shown me her new badge and freshly baked cookie. I'd turned onto the road, turned on her favorite music, and turned my attention to more sophisticated matters of schedules and obligations.

But only steps into the maze of thought I stepped back out. Sara was singing. Singing about

God. Singing to God. Head back, chin up, and lungs full, she filled the car with music. Heaven's harps paused to listen.

Is that my daughter? She sounds older. She looks older, taller, even prettier. Did I sleep through something? What happened to the chubby cheeks? What happened to the little face and pudgy fingers? She is becoming a young lady. Blonde hair down to her shoulders. Feet dangling over the seat. Somewhere in the night a page had turned and—well, look at her!

If you're a parent, you know what I mean. Just yesterday, diapers. Today, the car keys? Suddenly your child is halfway to the dormitory, and you're running out of chances to show your love, so you speak.

That's what I did. The song stopped, and Sara stopped, and I ejected the tape and put my hand on her shoulder and said, "Sara, you're something special." She turned and smiled tolerantly. "Someday some hairy-legged boy is going to steal your heart and sweep you into the next century. But right now, you belong to me."

She tilted her head, looked away for a minute, then looked back and asked, "Daddy, why are you acting so weird?"

I suppose such words would sound strange to a six-year-old. The love of a parent falls awkwardly on the ears of a child. My burst of emotion was beyond her. But that didn't keep me from speaking.

There is no way our little minds can comprehend the love of God. But that didn't keep him from coming.

And we, too, have tilted our heads. Like Sara, we have wondered what our Father was doing. From the cradle in Bethlehem to the cross in Jerusalem, we've pondered the love of our Father. What can you say to that kind of emotion? Upon learning that God would rather die than live without you, how do you react? How can you begin to explain such passion? If you're Paul the apostle, you don't. You make no statements. You offer no explanations. You ask a few questions.

These questions are not new to you. You've asked them before. In the night you've asked them; in anger you've asked them. The doctor's diagnosis brought them to the surface, as did the court's decision, the phone call from the bank, and the incomprehensible tragedies that occur in our world. The questions are probes of pain and problem and circumstance. No, the questions are not new, but maybe the answers are.

If God is for us, who can be against us? (Rom. 8:31 NIV)

The question is not simply "Who can be against us?" You could answer that one. Who is against you? Disease, inflation, corruption, exhaustion. Calamities confront, and fears imprison. Were Paul's question "Who can be against us?" we could list our foes much easier than we could fight them. But that is not the question. The question is, If God is for us, who can be against us?

Indulge me for a moment. Four words in this verse deserve your attention. Read slowly the phrase "God is for us." Please pause for a minute before you continue. Read it again, aloud. (My apologies to the person next to you.) *God is for us.* Repeat the phrase four times, this time emphasizing each word. (Come on, you're not in that big of a hurry.)

God is for us.

God *is* for us.

God is *for* us.

God is for *us*.

God is for you. Your parents may have forgotten you, your teachers may have neglected you, your siblings may be ashamed of you, but within reach of your prayers is the Maker of the oceans. God!

God *is* for you. Not "may be," not "has been," not "was," not "would be," but "God is"! He *is* for you. Today. At this hour. At this minute. As you read this sentence. No need to wait in line or come back tomorrow. He is with you. He could not be closer than he is at this second. His loyalty won't increase if you are better nor lessen if you are worse. He *is* for you.

God is *for* you. Turn to the sidelines; that's God cheering your run. Look past the finish line; that's God applauding your steps. Listen for him in the bleachers, shouting your name. Too tired to continue? He'll carry you. Too discouraged to fight? He's picking you up. God is *for* you.

God is for *you*. Had he a calendar, your birthday would be circled. If he drove a car, your name would be on his bumper. If there's a tree in heaven, he's carved your name in the bark. We know he has a tattoo, and we know what it says. "I have written your name on my hand," he declares (Isa. 49:16).

"Can a mother forget the baby at her breast and have no compassion on the child she has borne?" God asks in Isaiah 49:15 (NIV). What a bizarre question. Can you mothers imagine feeding your infant and then later asking, "What was that baby's name?" No. I've seen you care for your young. You stroke the hair, you touch the face, you sing the name over and over. Can a mother forget? No way. But "even if she could forget, I will not forget you," God pledges (Isa. 49:15).

God is with you. Knowing that, who is against you? Can death harm you now? Can disease rob your life? Can your purpose be taken or your value diminished? No. Though hell itself may set itself against you, no one can defeat you. You are protected. God is with you.

> He who did not spare his own Son, but gave him up for us all—how will he not also, along with him, graciously give us all things? (Rom. 8:32 NIV)

Suppose a man comes upon a child being beaten by thugs. He dashes into the mob, rescues the boy, and carries him to a hospital. The youngster is nursed to health. The man pays for the child's treatment. He learns that the child is an orphan and adopts him as his own and gives the boy his name. And then, one night months later, the father hears the son sobbing into his pillow. He goes to him and asks about the tears.

"I'm worried, Daddy. I'm worried about tomorrow. Where will I get food to eat? How am

I going to buy clothes to stay warm? And where will I sleep?"

The father is rightfully troubled. "Haven't I shown you? Don't you understand? I risked my life to save you. I gave my money to treat you. You wear my name. I've called you my son. Would I do all that and then not meet your needs?"

This is Paul's question. *Would he who gave his Son not meet our needs?*

But still we *worry*. We worry about the IRS and the SAT and the FBI. We worry about education, recreation, and constipation. We worry that we won't have enough money, and when we have money, we worry that we won't manage it well. We worry that the world will end before the parking meter expires. We worry what the dog thinks if he sees us step out of the shower. We worry that someday we'll learn that fat-free yogurt was fattening.

Honestly, now. Did God save you so you would

fret? Would he teach you to walk just to watch you fall? Would he be nailed to the cross for your sins and then disregard your prayers? Come on. Is Scripture teasing us when it says, "He has put his angels in charge of you to watch over you wherever you go" (Ps. 91:11)?

I don't think so either.

Can anything separate us from the love Christ has for us? (Rom. 8:35)

There it is. This is the question. Here is what we want to know. We want to know how long God's love will endure. Does God really love us forever? Not just on Easter Sunday when our shoes are shined and our hair is fixed. I want to know (deep within, don't we all really want to know?), how does God feel about me when I'm a jerk? Not when I'm peppy and positive and ready to tackle world hunger. Not then. I know how he feels about me then. Even I like me then.

I want to know how he feels about me when I snap at anything that moves, when my thoughts are gutter-level, when my tongue is sharp enough to slice a rock. How does he feel about me then?

And when bad things happen—does God care then? Does he love me in the midst of fear? Is he with me when danger lurks?

Will God stop loving me?

That's the question. That's the concern. Oh, you don't say it; you may not even know it. But I can see it on your faces. I can hear it in your words. Did I cross the line this week? Last Tuesday when I drank vodka until I couldn't walk . . . last Thursday when my business took me where I had no business being . . . last summer when I cursed the God who made me as I stood near the grave of the child he gave me?

Did I drift too far? Wait too long? Slip too much? Was I too uncertain? Too fearful? Too angry at the pain in this world?

That's what we want to know.

Can anything separate us from the love Christ has for us?

God answered our question before we asked it. So we'd see his answer, he lit the sky with a star. So we'd hear it, he filled the night with a choir. And so we'd believe it, he did what no man had ever dreamed; he became flesh and dwelt among us.

He placed his hand on the shoulder of humanity and said, "You're something special."

Untethered by time, he sees us all. From the backwoods of Virginia to the business district of London; from the Vikings to the astronauts; from the cave dwellers to the kings; from the hut builders to the finger pointers to the rock stackers;

he sees us. Vagabonds and ragamuffins all, he saw us before we were born.

And he loves what he sees. Flooded by emotion, overcome by pride, the Starmaker turns to us, one by one, and says, "You are my child. I love you dearly. I'm aware that someday you'll turn from me and walk away. But I want you to know, I've already provided you a way back."

And to prove it, he did something extraordinary.

Stepping from the throne, he removed his robe of light and wrapped himself in skin: pigmented, human skin. The light of the universe entered a dark, wet womb. He who angels worship nestled himself in the placenta of a peasant, was birthed into the cold night, and then slept on cow's hay.

Mary didn't know whether to give him milk or give him praise, but she gave him both since he was, as near as she could figure, hungry and holy.

Joseph didn't know whether to call him Junior

or Father. But in the end he called him Jesus, since that's what the angel said and since he didn't have the faintest idea what to name a God he could cradle in his arms.

Neither Mary nor Joseph said it as bluntly as my Sara, but don't you think their heads tilted and their minds wondered, *What in the world are you doing, God?* Or, better phrased, *God, what are you doing in the world?*

"Can anything make me stop loving you?" God asks. "Watch me speak your language, sleep on your earth, and feel your hurts. Behold the Maker of sight and sound as he sneezes, coughs, and blows his nose. You wonder if I understand how you feel? Look into the dancing eyes of the kid in Nazareth; that's God walking to school. Ponder the toddler at Mary's table; that's God spilling his milk.

"You wonder how long my love will last? Find your answer on a splintered cross, on a craggy hill.

That's me you see up there, your Maker, your God. Nail-stabbed and bleeding. Covered in spit and sin-soaked. That's your sin I'm feeling. That's your death I'm dying. That's your resurrection I'm living. That's how much I love you.

"Can anything come between you and me?" asks the firstborn Son.

Hear the answer and stake your future on the triumphant words of Paul: "I am sure that neither death nor life, nor angels, nor ruling spirits, nothing now, nothing in the future, no powers, nothing above us, nothing below us, nor anything else in the whole world will ever be able to separate us from the love of God that is in Christ Jesus our Lord" (Rom. 8:38–39).

3 EYES ON THE FATHER

It does us twice as much good to think about God as it does to think about anyone or anything else. God wants us to begin and end our prayers thinking of him. The more we focus up there, the more inspired we are down here.

Magnify. When you magnify an object, you enlarge it so that you can understand it. When we magnify God, we do the same. We enlarge our awareness of him so we can understand him more. This is exactly what happens when we worship—we take our minds off ourselves and set them on God. The emphasis is on him.

I love the way the final phrase of the Lord's Prayer is translated in *The Message* (Matt. 6:13):

> You're in charge!
> You can do anything you want!
> You're ablaze in beauty!
>   Yes. Yes. Yes.

Could it be any simpler? God is in charge! This concept is not foreign to us. When the restaurant waiter brings you a cold hamburger and a hot soda, you want to know who is in charge. When a young fellow wants to impress his girlfriend, he takes her down to the convenience store where he works and boasts, "Every night from five to ten o'clock, I'm in charge." We know what it means to be in charge of a restaurant or a store. But to be in charge of the universe? This is the claim of Jesus.

God raised him from death and set him on a throne in deep heaven, *in charge* of running the universe, everything from galaxies to governments, no name and no power exempt from his rule. And not just for the time being, but forever. He is *in charge* of it all, has the final word on everything. At the center of all this, Christ rules the church. (Eph. 1:20–22 MSG, emphasis mine)

There are many examples of Jesus' authority, but I'll just mention one of my favorites. Jesus and the disciples are in a boat crossing the Sea of Galilee. A storm arises suddenly, and what was placid becomes violent—monstrous waves rise out of the sea and slap the boat. Mark describes it clearly: "A furious squall came up, and the waves broke over the boat, so that it was nearly swamped" (Mark 4:37 NIV).

It's very important that you get an accurate

picture, so I'm going to ask you to imagine yourself in the boat. It's a sturdy vessel but no match for these ten-foot waves. It plunges nose first into the wall of water. The force of the waves dangerously tips the boat until the bow seems to be pointing straight at the sky. And just when you fear flipping over backward, the vessel pitches forward into the valley of another wave. A dozen sets of hands join yours in clutching the mast. All your shipmates have wet heads and wide eyes. You tune your ear for a calming voice, but all you hear are screams and prayers. All of a sudden it hits you—someone is missing. Where is Jesus? He's not at the mast. He's not grabbing the edge either. Where is he? Then you hear something—a noise . . . a displaced sound . . . as if someone is snoring. You turn and look, and there curled in the stern of the boat is Jesus, sleeping!

You don't know whether to be amazed or angry,

so you're both. How can he sleep at a time like this? Or as the disciples asked, "Teacher, don't you care if we drown?" (Mark 4:38 NIV).

The very storm that made the disciples panic made him drowsy. What put fear in their eyes put him to sleep. The boat was a tomb to the followers and a cradle to Christ. How could he sleep through the storm? Simple—he was in charge of it.

> He got up, rebuked the wind and said to the waves, "Quiet! Be still!" Then the wind died down and it was completely calm. He said to his disciples, "Why are you so afraid? Do you still have no faith?" (Mark 4:39–40 NIV)

Incredible. He doesn't chant a mantra or wave a wand. No angels are called; no help is needed. The raging water becomes a stilled sea, instantly. Immediate calm. Not a ripple. Not a drop. Not a gust. In a moment the sea goes from a churning torrent to a peaceful pond. The reaction of the disciples? Read it in verse 41: "They were in absolute awe, staggered. 'Who is this, anyway?' they asked. 'Wind and sea at his beck and call!'" (MSG).

They'd never met a man like this. The waves were his subjects, and the winds were his servants. And that was just the beginning of what his sea mates would witness. Before it was over, they would see fish jump into the boat, demons dive into pigs, cripples turn into dancers, and cadavers turn into living, breathing people. "He even gives orders to evil spirits and they obey him," the people proclaimed (Mark 1:27 NIV).

Is it any wonder the disciples were willing to die for Jesus? Never had they seen such power; never had they seen such glory. It was like—well, like the whole universe was his kingdom. You wouldn't have needed to explain this verse to them; they knew what it meant: "For thine is the kingdom, and the power, and the glory, for ever" (Matt. 6:13 KJV).

In fact, it was two of these rescued fishermen who would declare his authority most clearly. Listen to John: "Greater is he that is in you, than he that is in the world" (1 John 4:4 KJV). Listen to Peter: "Jesus has gone into heaven and is at God's right side ruling over angels, authorities, and powers" (1 Pet. 3:22).

It's only right that they declare his authority. It's only right that we do the same. And when we do, we state without question: the ruler of the universe rules our hearts.

4
GOOD TRIUMPHANT

How could God allow evil to bring destruction and loss into our lives? Why doesn't he protect us from the perpetrators of wicked and evil acts? Our hearts ache, our questions churn. And yet, we've seen goodness emerge from tragedy and pain . . . heroic deeds, selfless compassion, a one-for-all sense of community. Somehow in the midst of something evil, goodness fights to prevail.

Is it really possible that something evil could end up being used for good? To answer that question, we have to look back—back to the very beginning of Evil itself.

Twice in Scripture the curtain of time is pulled back, and we are granted a glimpse at the most foolish gamble in history. Satan was an angel who was not content to be near God; he had to be above God. Lucifer was not satisfied to give God worship; he wanted to occupy God's throne.

According to Ezekiel, both Satan's beauty and evil were unequaled among the angels:

> *You were an example of what was perfect,*
> > *full of wisdom and perfect in beauty.*
> *You had a wonderful life,*
> > *as if you were in Eden, the garden of God.*
> *Every valuable gem was on you . . .*
> > *You walked among the gems that shined like fire.*
> *Your life was right and good*
> > *from the day you were created,*
> > *until evil was found in you.* (Ezek. 28:12–15)

The angels, like humans, were made to serve and worship God. The angels, like humans, were given free will. Otherwise how could they worship? Both Isaiah and Ezekiel describe an angel more powerful than any human, more beautiful than any creature, yet more foolish than any being who has ever lived. His pride was his downfall.

Most scholars point to Isaiah 14:13–14 as the description of Lucifer's tumble:

> *I will go up to heaven.*
> *I will put my throne*
>   *above God's stars.*
> *I will sit on the mountain of the gods,*
>   *on the slopes of the sacred mountain.*
> *I will go up above the tops of the clouds.*
>   *I will be like God Most High.*

You can't miss the cadence of arrogance in the words: "I will . . . I will . . . I will . . . I will . . . I will." Because he sought to be like God, Satan fell away from God and has spent history trying to convince us to do the same. Isn't that the strategy he used with Eve? "You will be like God," he promised (Gen. 3:5).

He has not changed. He is as self-centered now as he was then. He is as foolish now as he was then. And he is just as limited now as he was then. Even when Lucifer's heart was good, he was inferior to God. All angels are inferior to God. God knows everything; they only know what he reveals. God is everywhere; they can be in only one place. God is all-powerful; angels are only as powerful as God allows them to be. All angels, including Satan, are inferior to God. And this may surprise you: Satan is still a servant to God.

He doesn't want to be. He doesn't intend to be.

He would like nothing more than to build his own kingdom, but he can't. Every time he tries to advance his cause, he ends up advancing God's.

Erwin Lutzer articulates this thought in his book *The Serpent of Paradise:*

> The devil is just as much God's servant in his rebellion as he was in the days of his sweet obedience . . . We can't quote Luther too often: The devil is God's devil.
>
> Satan has different roles to play, depending on God's counsel and purposes. He is pressed into service to do God's will in the world; he must do the bidding of the Almighty. We must bear in mind that he does have frightful powers, but knowing that those can only be exercised under God's direction and pleasure gives us hope. Satan is simply not free to wreak havoc on people at will.[1]

Satan doing the bidding of the Almighty? Seeking the permission of God? Does such language strike you as strange? It may. If it does, you can be sure Satan would rather you not hear what I'm about to say to you. He'd much rather you be deceived into thinking of him as an independent force with unlimited power. Satan has absolutely no power, except that power God permits.

He'd rather you never hear the words of John: "God's Spirit, who is in you, is greater than the devil, who is in the world" (1 John 4:4). And he'd certainly rather you never learn how God uses the devil as an instrument to advance the cause of Christ.

How does God use Satan to do the work of heaven? God uses Satan to:

1. *Refine the faithful.* We all have the devil's disease. Even the meekest among us have a tendency to think too highly of ourselves. Apparently the

apostle Paul did. His résumé was impressive: a personal audience with Jesus, a participant in heavenly visions, an apostle chosen by God, an author of the Bible. He healed the sick, traveled the world, and penned some of history's greatest documents. Few could rival his achievements. And maybe he knew it. Perhaps there was a time when Paul began to pat himself on the back. God, who loved Paul and hates pride, protected Paul from the sin. And he used Satan to do it.

To keep me from becoming conceited because of these surpassingly great revelations, there was given me a thorn in my flesh, a messenger of Satan, to torment me. (2 Cor. 12:7 NIV)

We aren't told the nature of the thorn, but we are told its purpose—to keep Paul humble. We are also told its origin—a messenger of Satan. The messenger could have been a pain, a problem, or a person who was a pain. We don't know. But we do know the messenger was under God's control. Please note what Paul says next:

Three times I pleaded with the Lord to take it away from me. But he said to me, "My grace is sufficient for you, for my power is made perfect in weakness." (vv. 8–9 NIV)

Satan and his forces were simply a tool in the hand of God to strengthen a servant.

Another example of the devil as God's servant is the temptation of Job. The devil dares to question the stability of Job's faith, and God gives him permission to test Job. "All right then," God says. "Everything Job has is in your power, but you must not touch Job himself" (Job 1:12). Note that God set both the permission and the parameters of the struggle. Job passes the test, and Satan complains, stating that Job would have fallen had he been forced to face pain. Again God gives permission, and again God gives the parameters. "Job is in your power," he tells Satan, "but you may not take his life" (2:6).

Though the pain and the questions are abundant, in the end Job's faith and health are greater than ever. Again, we may not understand the reason for the test, but we know its source. Read this verse out of the last chapter. The family of Job "comforted him and made him feel better about the trouble *the* LORD had brought on him" (42:11, emphasis mine).

Satan has no power except that which God gives him.

Even when Satan appears to win, he loses. Martin Luther was right on target when he described the devil as God's tool, a hoe used to care for his garden. The hoe never cuts what the Gardener intends to save and never saves what the Gardener intends to weed. Surely a part of Satan's punishment is the frustration he feels in unwillingly serving as a tool to create a garden for God. Satan is used by God to refine the faithful.

God also uses the devil to:

2. *Awaken the sleeping.* Hundreds of years before Paul, another Jewish leader battled with his ego, but he lost. Saul, the first king of Israel, was consumed with jealousy. He was upstaged by David, the youngest son of a shepherding family. David did everything better than Saul: he sang better, he impressed the women more, he even killed the giants Saul feared. But rather than celebrate David's God-given abilities, Saul grew insanely hostile. God, in an apparent effort to awaken Saul from this fog of jealousy, enlisted the help of his unwilling servant, Satan. "The next day an evil

spirit from God rushed upon Saul, and he prophesied in his house" (1 Sam. 18:10).

Observe a solemn principle: there are times when hearts grow so hard and ears so dull that God turns us over to endure the consequences of our choices. In this case, the demon was released to torment Saul. If Saul would not drink from the cup of God's kindness, let him spend some time drinking from the cup of hell's fury. "Let him be driven to despair that he might be driven back into the arms of God."[2]

The New Testament refers to incidents where similar discipline was administered. Paul chastises the church in Corinth for their tolerance of immorality. About an adulterer in the church he says: "Then hand this man over to Satan. So his sinful self will be destroyed, and his spirit will be saved on the day of the Lord" (1 Cor. 5:5).

Another example of such action is the case of

Hymenaeus and Alexander, two disciples who had made a shipwreck of their faith and negatively influenced others. "I have given them to Satan," Paul tells Timothy, "so they will learn not to speak against God" (1Tim. 1:20).

As drastic as it may appear, God will actually allow a person to experience hell on earth, in hopes of awakening his faith. A holy love makes the tough choice to release the child to the consequences of his rebellion.

By the way, doesn't this help explain the rampant evil that exists in the world? If God allows us to endure the consequences of our sin, and the world is full of sinners, then the world is going to abound in evil. Isn't this what Paul meant in the first chapter of Romans? After describing those who worship the creation rather than the Creator, Paul says, "God left them and let them do the shameful things they wanted to do" (Rom. 1:26).

Does God enjoy seeing the heartbreak and addictions of his children? No more than a parent enjoys disciplining a child. But holy love makes tough choices.

Remember, discipline should result in mercy, not misery. Some saints are awakened by a tap on the shoulder, while others need a two-by-four to the head. And whenever God needs a two-by-four, Satan gets the call.

He also gets the call to:

3. *Teach the church.* Perhaps the clearest illustration of how God uses Satan to achieve his purposes is found in the life of Peter. Listen to the warning Jesus gives to him: "Simon, Simon, Satan has asked to test all of you as a farmer sifts his wheat. I have prayed that you will not lose your faith! Help your brothers be stronger when you come back to me" (Luke 22:31–32).

Again, notice who is in control. Even though

Satan had a plan, he had to get permission. "All authority in heaven and on earth has been given to me," Jesus explained, and this is proof (Matt. 28:18 NIV). The wolf cannot get to the sheep without the permission of the Shepherd, and the Shepherd will only permit the attack if, in the long term, the pain is worth the gain.

The purpose of this test is to provide a testimony for the church. Jesus was allowing Peter to experience a trial so he could encourage his brothers. Perhaps God is doing the same with you. God knows that the church needs living testimonies of his power. Your difficulty, your disease, your conflict are preparing you to be a voice of encouragement to your brothers. All you need to remember is:

No test or temptation that comes your way is beyond the course of what others have had to face. All you need to remember is that God will never let you down; he'll never let you be pushed past your limit; he'll always be there to help you come through it. (1 Cor. 10:13 MSG)

You meant evil against me, but God meant it for good. (Gen. 50:20 NASB)

THE BITTER TASTE
OF REVENGE

Justice or revenge? It is justice that demands those who do evil against our society must be punished by our society. But justice is much different from revenge. Revenge is a matter of the heart. Revenge says, "Just you wait. I'll get you."

When we're hurt or offended, it doesn't take long to find ourselves wanting payment from those who are indebted to us.

Doesn't someone owe you something? An apology? A second chance? A fresh start? An explanation? A thank you? A childhood? A marriage? Stop and think about it (which I don't encourage you to do for long), and you can make a list of a lot of folks who are in your debt. Your parents should have been more protective. Your children should have been more appreciative. Your spouse should be more sensitive. Your preacher should have been more attentive.

What are you going to do with those in your debt? People in your past have dipped their hands into your purse and taken what was yours. What are you going to do? Few questions are more important. Dealing with debt is at the heart of your happiness.

Jesus said, "For if you forgive men when they sin against you, your heavenly Father will also forgive you. But if you do not forgive men their sins, your Father will not forgive your sins" (Matt. 6:14–15 NIV).

Jesus does not question the reality of your wounds. He does not doubt that you have been sinned against. The issue is not the existence of pain; the issue is the treatment of pain. What are you going to do with your debts?

Dale Carnegie tells about a visit to Yellowstone Park, where he saw a grizzly bear. The huge animal was in the center of a clearing, feeding on some discarded camp food. For several minutes he feasted alone; no other creature dared draw near. After a few moments a skunk walked through the meadow toward the food and took his place next to the grizzly. The bear didn't object, and Carnegie knew why. "The grizzly," he said, "knew the high cost of getting even."[1]

We'd be wise to learn the same. Settling the score is done at great expense.

For one thing, you pay a price relationally.

Have you ever noticed in the Western movies how the bounty hunter travels alone? It's not hard to see why. Who wants to hang out with a guy who settles scores for a living? Who wants to risk getting on his bad side? More than once I've heard a person spew his anger. He thought I was listening, when really I was thinking, *I hope I never get on his list*. Cantankerous sorts, these bounty hunters. Best leave them alone. Hang out with the angry, and you might catch a stray bullet. Debt settling is a lonely occupation. It's also an unhealthy occupation.

You pay a high price physically.

The Bible says it best: "Resentment kills a fool" (Job 5:2 NIV). It reminds me of an old Amos and Andy routine. Amos asks Andy what that little bottle is he's wearing around his neck. "Nitroglycerin," he answers. Amos is stunned that Andy would be wearing a necklace of nitro, so he asks for an explanation. Andy tells him about a fellow who has a bad habit of poking people in the chest while he's speaking. "It drives me crazy," Andy says. "I'm wearing this nitro so the next time he pokes me, I'll blow his finger off."

Andy's not the first to forget that when you try to get even, you get hurt. Job was right when he said, "You tear yourself to pieces in your anger" (Job 18:4). Ever notice that we describe the people who bug us as a "pain in the neck"? Whose neck are we referring to? Certainly not theirs. We are the ones who suffer.

If you're out to settle the score, you'll never rest. How can you? For one thing, your enemy may never pay up. As much as you think you deserve an apology, your debtor may not agree. The racist may never repent. The chauvinist may never change. As justified as you are in your quest for vengeance, you may never get a penny's worth of justice. And if you do, will it be enough?

Let's really think about this one. How much justice is enough? Picture your enemy for a moment.

Picture him tied to the whipping post. The strong-armed man with the whip turns to you and asks, "How many lashes?" And you give a number. The whip cracks and the blood flows and the punishment is inflicted. Your foe slumps to the ground, and you walk away.

Are you happy now? Do you feel better? Are you at peace? Perhaps for a while, but soon another memory will surface, and another lash will be needed, and . . . when does it all stop?

It stops when you take seriously the words of Jesus: "For if you forgive men when they sin against you, your heavenly Father will also forgive you. But if you do not forgive men their sins, your Father will not forgive your sins" (Matt. 6:14–15 NIV).

"Treat me as I treat my neighbor." Are you aware that this is what you are saying to your Father? "Give me what I give them. Grant me the same peace I grant others. Let me enjoy the same tolerance I offer." God will treat you the way you treat others.

Would you like some peace? Then quit giving your neighbor such a hassle. Want to enjoy God's generosity? Then let others enjoy yours. Would you like assurance that God forgives you? I think you know what you need to do.

6

IN THE SILENCE,
GOD SPEAKS

When we're hurting, sometimes we find healing by talking about it—with a friend, a counselor, to God. But eventually, the time comes to stop talking and listen.

There are times when to speak is to violate the moment . . . when silence represents the highest respect. The word for such times is *reverence*.

This was a lesson Job learned—the man in the Bible most touched by tragedy and despair. If Job had a fault, it was his tongue. He talked too much.

Not that anyone could blame him. Calamity had pounced on the man like a lioness on a herd of gazelles, and by the time the rampage passed, there was hardly a wall standing or a loved one living. Enemies had slaughtered Job's cattle, and lightning had destroyed his sheep. Strong winds had left his partying kids buried in wreckage.

Job knew what it was like to lose those he loved when the building collapsed.

Job hadn't even had time to bury his children before he saw the leprosy on his hands and the boils on his skin. His wife, compassionate soul that she was, told him to "curse God and die." His four friends came with the bedside manner of drill sergeants, telling him that God is fair, and pain is the result of evil, and as sure as two plus two equals four, Job must have some criminal record in his past to suffer so.

Each had his own interpretation of God, and each spoke long and loud about who God is and why God had done what he had done. They weren't the only ones talking about God. When his accusers paused, Job gave his response. Back and forth they went . . .

Job cried out . . . (3:1)

Then Eliphaz the Temanite answered . . . (4:1)

Then Job answered . . . (6:1)

Then Bildad the Shuhite answered . . . (8:1)

Then Job answered . . . (9:1)

Then Zophar the Naamathite answered . . . (11:1)

This verbal ping-pong continues for twenty-three chapters. Finally Job has enough of this "answering." No more discussion-group chitchat. It's time for the keynote address. He grips the microphone with one hand and the pulpit with the other and launches forth. For six chapters Job gives his opinions on God. This time the chapter headings read: "And Job continued," "And Job continued,"

"And Job continued." He defines God, explains God, and reviews God. One gets the impression that Job knows more about God than God does!

We are thirty-seven chapters into the book before God clears his throat to speak. Chapter 38 begins with these words: "Then the LORD answered Job."

If your Bible is like mine, there is a mistake in this verse. The words are fine, but the typesetter used the wrong size type. The words should look like this:

THEN THE LORD ANSWERED JOB!

God speaks. Faces turn toward the sky. Winds bend the trees. Neighbors plunge into the storm shelters. Cats scurry up the trees, and dogs duck into the bushes. "Somethin's a-blowin' in, honey. Best get them sheets off the line." God has no more than opened his mouth before Job knows he should have kept his sore one shut.

I will ask you questions,
  and you must answer me.
Where were you when I made the earth's foundation?
  Tell me, if you understand.
Who marked off how big it should be?
  Surely you know!
  Who stretched a ruler across it?
What were the earth's foundations set on,
  or who put its cornerstone in place
while the morning stars sang together
  and all the angels shouted with joy? (38:3–7)

God floods the sky with queries, and Job cannot help but get the point: only God defines God. You've got to know the alphabet before you can read, and God tells Job, "You don't even know the ABCs of heaven, much less the vocabulary." For the first time, Job is quiet. Silenced by a torrent of questions.

Have you ever gone to where the sea begins
or walked in the valleys under the sea?
Have you ever gone into the storehouse of the snow
or seen the storehouses for hail?
Job, are you the one who gives the horse its strength
or puts a flowing mane on its neck?
Do you make the horse jump like a locust?
Is it through your wisdom that the hawk flies
and spreads its wings toward the south? (38:16,
22; 39:19–20, 26)

Job barely has time to shake his head at one
question before he is asked another. The Father's
implication is clear: "As soon as you are able to
handle these simple matters of storing stars and
stretching the neck of the ostrich, then we'll have a
talk about pain and suffering. But until then, we
can do without your commentary."

Does Job get the message? I think so. Listen to his response.

I am not worthy; I cannot answer you anything,
  so I will put my hand over my mouth. (40:4)

Notice the change. Before he heard God, Job couldn't speak enough. After he heard God, he couldn't speak at all.

Silence was the only proper response. There was a time in the life of Thomas à Kempis when he, too, covered his mouth. He had written profusely about the character of God. But one day God confronted him with such holy grace that, from that moment on, all à Kempis's words "seemed like straw." He put down his pen and never wrote another line. He put his hand over his mouth.

The word for such moments is *reverence*.

Jesus taught us to pray with reverence when he

modeled for us "Hallowed be your name." This phrase is a petition, not a proclamation. A request, not an announcement. "Be hallowed, Lord." Do whatever it takes to be holy in my life. Take your rightful place on the throne. Exalt yourself. Magnify yourself. Glorify yourself. You be Lord, and I'll be quiet.

The word *hallowed* comes from the word *holy,* and the word *holy* means "to separate." The ancestry of the term can be traced back to an ancient word that means "to cut." To be holy, then, is to be a cut above the norm, superior, extraordinary. The Holy One dwells on a different level from the rest of us. What frightens us does not frighten him. What troubles us does not trouble him.

I'm more a landlubber than a sailor, but I've puttered around in a bass boat enough to know the secret for finding land in a storm . . . You don't aim at another boat. You certainly don't stare at the waves. You set your sights on an object unaffected by the wind—a light on the shore—and go straight toward it. The light is unaffected by the storm.

By seeking God, you do the same. When you set your sights on our God, you focus on One who can overcome any storm life may bring.

Like Job, you find peace in the pain.

Like Job, you cover your mouth and sit still.

"Be still, and know that I am God" (Ps. 46:10 NIV). This verse contains a command with a promise.

The command? *Be still. Cover your mouth. Bend your knees.*

The promise? *You will know that I am God.*

The vessel of faith journeys on soft waters. Belief rides on the wings of waiting.

In the midst of your daily storms, and in this storm that has swept over our country and even the entire world, make it a point to be still and set your sights on him. Let God be God. Let him bathe you in his glory so that both your breath and your troubles are sucked from your soul. Be still. Be quiet. Be open and willing. Take a moment to be still, and know that he is God.

7
IN THE STORM,
WE PRAY

When disasters strike, the human spirit responds by reaching out to help those affected. People stand in line to give blood. Millions of dollars are donated to aid victims and their families. Rescue teams work for endless hours. But the most essential effort is accomplished by another valiant team. Their task? To guard and gird the world with prayer. Those who pray keep alive the watch fires of faith. For the most part, we don't even know their names. Such is the case of someone who prayed on a day long ago.

His name is not important. His looks are

immaterial. His gender is of no concern. His title is irrelevant. He is important not because of who he was, but because of what he did.

He went to Jesus on behalf of a friend. His friend was sick, and Jesus could help, and someone needed to go to Jesus, so someone went. Others cared for the sick man in other ways. Some brought food; others provided treatment; still others comforted the family. Each role was crucial. Each person was helpful, but no one was more vital than the one who went to Jesus.

John writes: "So Mary and Martha sent *someone* to tell Jesus, 'Lord, the one you love is sick'" (John 11:3, emphasis mine).

Someone carried the request. Someone walked the trail. Someone went to Jesus on behalf of Lazarus. And because someone went, Jesus responded.

In the economy of heaven, the prayers of saints

are a valued commodity. John the apostle would
agree. He wrote the story of Lazarus and was care-
ful to show the sequence: the healing began when
the request was made.

The phrase the friend of Lazarus used is worth
noting. When he told Jesus of the illness, he said,
"Lord, the one you love is sick." He didn't base his
appeal on the imperfect love of the one in need but
on the perfect love of the Savior. He didn't say,
"The one *who loves you* is sick." He said, "The
one *you love* is sick." The power of the prayer, in
other words, does not depend on the one who
makes the prayer but on the one who hears the
prayer.

We can and must repeat the phrase in manifold
ways. "The one you love is tired, sad, hungry,
lonely, fearful, depressed." The words of the prayer
vary, but the response never changes. The Savior
hears the prayer. He silences heaven so he won't

miss a word. He hears the prayer. Remember the phrase from John's gospel? "When Jesus *heard* this, he said, 'This sickness will not end in death'" (John 11:4, emphasis mine).

The Master heard the request. Jesus stopped whatever he was doing and took note of the man's words. This anonymous courier was heard by God.

You and I live in a loud world. To get someone's attention is no easy task. He must be willing to set everything aside to listen: turn down the radio, turn away from the monitor, turn the corner of the page and set down the book. When someone is willing to silence everything else so he can hear us clearly, it is a privilege. A rare privilege indeed.

So John's message is critical. You can talk to God because God listens. Your voice matters in heaven. He takes you very seriously. When you enter his presence, the attendants turn to you to hear your voice. No need to fear that you will be ignored. Even if you stammer or stumble, even if what you have to say impresses no one, it impresses God—and he listens. He listens to the painful plea of the elderly in the rest home. He listens to the gruff confession of the death-row inmate. When the alcoholic begs for mercy, when the spouse seeks guidance, when the businessman steps off the street into the chapel, God listens.

Intently. Carefully. The prayers are honored as precious jewels. Purified and empowered, the words rise in a delightful fragrance to our Lord. "The smoke from the incense went up from the angel's hand to God" (Rev. 8:4). Incredible. Your words do not stop until they reach the very throne of God.

One call and heaven's fleet appears. Your prayer on earth activates God's power in heaven.

You are the someone of God's kingdom. Your prayers move God to change the world. You may not understand the mystery of prayer. You don't need to. But this much is clear: actions in heaven begin when someone prays on earth. What an amazing thought!

When you speak, Jesus hears.

And when Jesus hears, the world is changed.

All because someone prayed.

8 FROM GOD'S PERSPECTIVE

We don't like to say good-bye to those we love. But we have to. Try as we might to avoid it, as reluctant as we are to discuss it, death is a very real part of life. Eventually each one of us must release the hand of one we love into the hand of One we have not seen.

Can you remember the first time death forced you to say good-bye? Most of us can. I can. When I was in the third grade, I came home from school one day surprised to see my father's truck in the driveway. I found him in his bathroom, shaving. "Your Uncle Buck died today," he said. His announcement made me feel sad. I liked my uncle. I didn't know him well, but I liked him. The news also made me curious.

At the funeral I heard words like *departed, passed on, gone ahead*. These were unfamiliar terms. I wondered, *Departed to where? Passed on to what? Gone ahead for how long?*

Of course, I've learned since that I'm not the only one with questions about death. Listen in on any discussion about the return of Christ, and someone will inquire, "But what about those who have already died? What happens to Christians between their death and Jesus' return?"

Apparently the church in Thessalonica asked such a question. Listen to the apostle Paul's words to them from 1 Thessalonians: "We want you to be quite certain, brothers, about those who have died, to make sure that you do not grieve about them, like the other people who have no hope" (4:13 JB).

The Thessalonian church had buried her share of loved ones. And the apostle wanted the members who remained to be at peace regarding the ones who had gone ahead. Many of you have buried loved ones as well. And just as God spoke to them, he speaks to you.

If you'll celebrate a marriage anniversary alone this year, he speaks to you.

If your child made it to heaven before making it to kindergarten, he speaks to you.

If you lost a loved one in violence, if you learned more than you want to know about disease, if your dreams were buried as they lowered the casket, God speaks to you.

He speaks to all of us who have stood or will stand in the soft dirt near an open grave. And to us he gives this confident word: "I want you to know what happens to a Christian when he dies so that when it happens, you will not be full of sorrow, as those who have no hope. For since we believe that Jesus died and then came back to life again, we can also believe that when Jesus returns, God will bring back with him all the Christians who have died" (1 Thess. 4:13–14 TLB).

God transforms our hopeless grief into hope-filled grief. How? By telling us that we will see our loved ones again.

Isn't that what we want to believe? We long to know that our loved ones are safe in death. We long for the reassurance that the soul goes immediately to be with God. But dare we believe it? Can we believe it? According to the Bible we can.

Scripture is surprisingly quiet about this phase of our lives. When speaking about the period between the death of the body and the resurrection of the body, the Bible doesn't shout; it just whispers. But at the confluence of these whispers, a firm voice is heard. This authoritative voice assures us that at

death the Christian immediately enters into the presence of God and enjoys conscious fellowship with
the Father and with those who have gone before.

Where do I get such ideas? Listen to some of the
whispers:

For to me, to live is Christ and to die is gain. If I
am to go on living in the body, this will mean
fruitful labor for me. Yet what shall I choose? I do
not know! I am torn between the two: I desire to
depart and be with Christ, which is better by far.
(Phil. 1:21–23 NIV)

The language here suggests an immediate depar-
ture of the soul after death. The details of the
grammar are a bit tedious but led one scholar to
suggest: "What Paul is saying here is that the
moment he departs or dies, that very moment he is
with the Christ."[1]

Another clue comes from the letter Paul wrote to the Corinthians. Perhaps you've heard the phrase "to be absent from the body is to be at home with the Lord"? Paul used it first in 2 Corinthians 5:8: "We really want to be away from this body and be at home with the Lord."

We don't like to say good-bye to those we love. But if what the Bible says about heaven is true, and I believe it is, then the ultimate prayer, the ultimate answered prayer, is heaven.

It is right for us to weep, but there is no need for us to despair. They had pain here. They have no pain there. They struggled here. They have no struggles there. You and I might wonder why God took them home. But they don't. They understand. They are, at this very moment, at peace in the presence of God.

DO IT AGAIN, LORD
A Prayer for Troubled Times

DEAR LORD,

We're still hoping we'll wake up. We're still hoping we'll open a sleepy eye and think, *What a horrible dream. How could this have happened?*

We are sad, Father.

And so we come to you. We don't ask you for help; we beg you for it. We don't request; we implore. We know what you can do. We've read the accounts. We've pondered the stories, and now we plead, "Do it again, Lord. Do it again."

Remember Joseph? You rescued him from the pit. You can do the same for us. Do it again, Lord.

Remember the Hebrews in Egypt? You protected their children from the angel of death. We have children too, Lord. Do it again.

And Sarah? Remember her prayers? You heard them. Joshua? Remember his fears? You inspired him. The women at the tomb? You resurrected their hope. The doubts of Thomas? You took them away. Do it again, Lord. Do it again.

You changed Daniel from a captive into a king's counselor. You took Peter the fisherman and made him Peter an apostle. Because of you, David went from leading sheep to leading armies. Do it again, Lord, for we need counselors today. We need apostles. We need leaders. Do it again, dear Lord.

Most of all, do again what you did at Calvary. What we saw in this tragedy, you saw there on that Friday. Innocence ended. Goodness suffering. Mothers weeping. Evil dancing. Just as the shadows fell on our children, the darkness fell on your Son. Just as our world has been shattered, the very child of Eternity was pierced.

And by dusk, heaven's sweetest song was silent, buried behind a rock.

But you did not waver, O Lord. You did not waver. After your Son lay three days in a dark hole, you rolled the rock and rumbled the earth and turned the darkest Friday into the brightest Sunday. Do it again, Lord. Turn this Calvary into an Easter.

Thank you for these hours of prayer.

Let your mercy be upon all who suffer. Grant to those who lead us wisdom beyond their years and experience. Have mercy upon the souls who have departed and the wounded who remain. Give us grace that we might forgive and faith that we might believe.

And look kindly upon your church. For two thousand years you've used her to heal a hurting world.

Do it again, Lord. Do it again.

Through Christ, amen.[1]

Notes

Chapter Four: *Good Triumphant*
1. Erwin Lutzer, *The Serpent of Paradise* (Chicago: Moody Press, 1996), 102.
2. Ibid., 111.

Chapter Five: *The Bitter Taste of Revenge*
1. John MacArthur, "The Pardon of Prayer" audiotape (Panorama City, Calif.: Word of Grace, 1980).

Chapter Eight: *From God's Perspective*
1. Anthony Hoekema, *The Bible and the Future* (Grand Rapids: Eerdmans, 1979), 104.

Do It Again, Lord: *A Prayer for Troubled Times*
1. Adapted from a prayer written for America Prays, a national prayer vigil on September 15, 2001.

ABOUT THE AUTHOR

MAX LUCADO has a blessed calling:

Denalyn calls him Honey.

Jenna, Andrea, and Sara call him Dad.

The folks at the Oak Hills Church in San Antonio
call him their preacher.

And God calls him His.

Not bad, huh?

Also Available from Max Lucado